How Retail Businesses Can Innovate and Adapt to the New Normal

A huge number of small businesses across the globe are confronted with the comparative test of survival, as a result of the pandemic lockdown, A significant part of the economy and buyers remained at home to moderate the spread of the infection. To remain above the situation, business owners adapted on the fly and discovered inventive approaches to change their working models.

All things considered, numerous retail businesses have fizzled. Others have endured and plan to utilize experiences observed during the pandemic to drive income and create new opportunities as the economy recuperates. However, the effect on a large number of workers generally is uncertain.

Retail-business attempting to survive the coronavirus pandemic will be confronted by a financial blow more than at any time in recent history.

Retail businesses have been downsizing and temporarily shutting down as buyers remain at home to curtail the spread of the exceptionally irresistible infection, otherwise called COVID-19. Without accessing funds, numerous small businesses—particularly retailers and shops on the Streets—will before long have to chop staff or closed down for good.

Examples of Small Businesses:

Restaurants

Repair and maintenance

Retailers

Construction

Personal services

Manufacturing

Restaurant

Fitness

Unique Business Model For Retail Business Growth

Innovation and planning is a critical factors for Retail organizations to endure and proceed until the pandemic is finished. Retailers should exploit this extraordinary beginning and push for growth.

Strategy for adapting to the new normal include:

- Host small-scale seminars on Zoom that offer your customers critical thinking tips.
- Get invited to speak at other people's online masterclasses and webinars.
- Host roundtables on Zoom on a topic, invite other entrepreneurs; and post to YouTube.
- Request invitations to speak at online events.
- Participate in networking opportunities at the events like breakout rooms.

- Solicit invitations to speak on other people's podcasts.
- Host virtual meetings for coffee over Zoom with people.
- Professional and business connections via LinkedIn.
- Offer free strategy calls to prospects and clients
- Join a mastermind group with other entrepreneurs that meet online
- Volunteer with associations to help them stage online events (committee meetings are networking opportunities)

Go Digital

With numerous business activities going virtual in the early months of the pandemic, customary small businesses were forced to break new ground to keep up with marketing projections. A critical factor for businesses that endure the pandemic with insignificant harm to income were those that immediately adapted to an online platform.

Social media is largely affecting small businesses during this time. Building up a few social media pages (Facebook, Instagram, or Twitter) where your current and planned clients can reach you and view items and services is an additional advantage. An eye-getting website and dynamic social media support that is easy to use and outwardly engaging will help increment your online business.

COVID-19 dramatically affected small businesses by hampering growth and profitability. Be that as it may, proprietors and entrepreneurs acted by moving activities internet, adapting their marketing, looking for new financing opportunities, or in any event, beginning something new. In short, they figured out how to endure and flourish.

Key Digital Strategy For Retail Growth

- Advertising and selling through social media like Whatsapp, Instagram, Facebook, and so forth.
- Reducing publicizing expenses.
- Publicizing and selling through email.

- Adding online business features to the website.
- Advertising and selling through other platforms such as online masterclass, youtube marketing, affiliate marketing, software apps, and email list database.

Explore Social Media and Digital Marketing

Focus on social media and email to reach clients. The coronavirus pandemic forced numerous simple organizations to accept computerized technology, for example, contactless payment instruments and internet booking software. Examination and reviews have shown that more small entrepreneurs are prioritizing social media and email to advance their items and services, much over their Retailers' websites.

However, businesses needn't bother with a complete computerized strategy—or even a website—to succeed on the web. An Alignable review tracked down that 25% of respondents were going to social media to arrive at clients while 18% were drawing in them through email marketing.

Renegotiate terms of contracts and debt
Retail business owners should ask landlords for more an ideal opportunities to pay their lease, for instance. They ought to likewise ask banks to temporarily concede revenue installments on outstanding debt.

Reduce every cost

Each dollar matters now. Organizations barely holding on should attempt to renew contracts with business partners and landlords, and refinance debt.

Concentrate on the best profit opportunities

Small entrepreneurs should recognize their most significant products and services and eliminate all the other things.

It's similarly important for firms to understand their generally faithful and profitable clients—what their identity is, the thing that they purchase, and how to draw in them to win their loyalty.

Technology To Help Retail businesses grow

Technology is the new normal in today's business world. The economy of world powers is driven by technology and science.

Retailers should digitize most of their products or services, and start offering them online to their customers and potential clients. Software technology such as Finance Data Analysis, be put in place to balance any loss of earnings by offering new ways to connect with customers.

Finance Data Analysis: Helps in digging deep into the financial data infrastructure to solve unique unilinear problems and tackle complex corner cases. Supports the writing ETLs (extract, transform, and load) to take data from various data sources (Python, SQL) and consolidate it into a single, centralized location. As well as identifying potential areas of automation within the Finance team.

Artificial Intelligence: AI can meet up customer service demand and satisfaction via chatbots by fully automating the process.

Web Development team: Retailers should create a web Development team to scale up and evolve their business. The developer should use WordPress and other web-diverse properties such as PHP, HTML, CSS, JavaScript, XML, and jQuery to evolve the retail business.

Data Science

Data science is a trending technology that can help retailers to find when and where their products sell best. With data science, Retailers can predict the success rate of their strategies.

The importance of data science helps businesses reduce costs, speed up service delivery, and generate forecasts for more effective decision-making. Data science helps to bridge the gap between the theoretical and the practical.

A data scientist should execute Artificial Intelligence theories from various Machine Learning (ML) models and algorithms to automate the Retailers' Business. There are many tools and software skills required for data science analysis such as data mining, machine learning, deep learning, statistical modeling, and data visualization techniques using data-oriented tools and languages such as Python, R, and MATLAB as well as programming languages (Python, R, Scala, Java, C/C++, C#).

Information Technology

I.T. in a business environment especially for Retailers will provide services such as computing technology, such as networking, hardware, software, the Internet; Desk support of IT services. This includes customer service, and support tracking documentation of IT services to include requests related to laptops and desktops, mobile devices, software installations, networking, and application support.

The Roles of Technology Expert include:

- Apply software and Hardware upgrades/security patches
- Printer/Copier support and Administration
- Shipping equipment installation and support
- Administration and support of Security camera systems
- Category 5/6 Cable management and rack installations
- Administration of Shortel VOIP phone system
- Office 365 user support and installations

- WebEx Teleconferencing support and Administration
- Office Wireless system support and administration

Role of Large Corporations to Small Businesses in Their Industry

Large corporations can mentor and loan money to smaller organizations like retailers. This memorandum of understanding has benefits for the two sides.

The survival pace of new businesses is understandably scary to entrepreneurs, however, those numbers can change radically when you add a mentor to the condition.

Beginning a small or medium-sized business implies you don't have a manager above you who provisions representative inspiration and commitment programs, which can be indispensable for worker joy and achievement. A mentor can often make up for this shortcoming, going about as a mentor to offer help, inspiration, approval, and consolation.

A decent small business mentor can help characterize basic undertakings and guide your business objectives - and more importantly, help the organization consider itself responsible for meeting them. In addition to the fact that accountability helps organizations meet these objectives toward progress, it likewise encourages a culture of independence and self-assurance.

A mentor brings their network of important individuals, and those contacts could be available to you. Do you have a specific business problem? A mentor may know the ideal individual to go to for help. Searching for the ideal individual for a new job in the organization? They could likewise suggest a contact from their experience in the industry.

Employee turnover

The worth of cheerful workers can't be downplayed and mentored employees bring about less turnover inside the organization. A sense of participation within employees prompts a feeling of possession and responsibility inside the organization and submitted representatives are more liable to be steadfast workers. A worker who is faithful and submitted will be more connected with and put resources into the accomplishment of your organization. Set aside the effort to establish an inclusive environment and motivates workers to take on projects that go past their present place of employment description.

Leadership is a Product of Mentorship

A leader tells you the best way to push the limits, to be inventive, to work standards and behavior, and to establish the vibe for your future work ethics.

Preparing ability is the only way for any business to arrive at its actual potential. Be specific when recruiting and search for representatives whose vision is lined up with yours and for candidates that will be open to training and mentorship.

Where to find a mentor:
- Local networking events
- Small Business Development Centers

- The Association of Women's Business Centers
- Professional and trade associations
- Social media: Don't neglect your, network when it comes to finding a mentor. LinkedIn and Twitter can be great resources for connecting with other professionals and potential mentors.

At the point when an entrepreneur sets up a business and is searching for help, most will be uninformed of how a business incubator can help, notwithstanding, that the benefits are clear. Shared learning, mentorship, quicker admittance to financing and the different subsidizing awards that are on offer and office space are generally indispensable for any new beginning up and, when you are launching a new business, benefits like these can put you in front of the opposition to appreciate sped up growth later on.

Retailers can be incubated by applying for government and Large Business Administration loans.

The weakest businesses will not keep going that long. They'll require revenue free loans and other money cushions to pay their workers and keep their storefronts.

The government additionally needs to do its part and broaden help efforts. Loans can assist numerous businesses with getting temporary closures and lift the organization's financial stability.

Benefits of Incubators To Small-scale Industry

- Incubators may likewise offer business development programmings, for example, workshops and board conversations.
- Your incubator ought to give a free or minimal effort workspace that permits you to reduce overhead while you grow.
- Search for an incubator that will give your business admittance to benefits that can help speed up your business, including office space and services,

mentorship, mastery, impact, and now and then capital.

- Businesses in certain incubators may approach office absolute necessities like the web, regulatory support, and creation hardware. Office services fluctuate from one program to another.
- Ensure investors trust the incubator to put resources into the correct new companies and man of the hour them into effective businesses. Joining this sort of incubator will give you a benefit when looking for financing.
- The structured environment and educational plan of an incubator can help

a new business stay on track and grow the correct way.

Research has it that Retail incubator companies experience very healthy growth with more rapid sales with the assistance of incubator than without one.

In conclusion, businesses that go through incubator and mentorship programs are also able to benefit from the reputation of those programs and the previous industries that have gone through those programs.

www.ingramcontent.com/pod-product-compliance
Lightning Source LLC
Chambersburg PA
CBHW080440220526
45465CB00009B/3369